Battling the Spirit of Perversion

To prevail and conquer

By: Anastasia "Stacie" Peart

Copyright © 2008 by Anastasia "Stacie" Peart

Battling the Spirit of Perversion
To prevail and conquer
by Anastasia "Stacie" Peart

Printed in the United States of America

ISBN 978-1-60477-466-5

All rights reserved solely by the author. The author guarantees all contents are original and do not infringe upon the legal rights of any other person or work. No part of this book may be reproduced in any form without the permission of the author. The views expressed in this book are not necessarily those of the publisher.

Unless otherwise indicated, Bible quotations are taken from the King James version, and the Amplified Bible, Copyright © 1995 by the Zonderland Corporation.

www.xulonpress.com

ACKNOWLEDGMENTS

First and foremost, I would thank the Most High God for the writing of this book. He was the *author* and I was the scribe. I once heard Prophetess Linda Abernathy say that "God doesn't allow things to happen to us for our misery; He does it for our ministry."

I'd like to thank my leader, my pastor... Dr. Apostle Aretha Wilson of Humble Heart Fellowship Ministries. She is indeed a mother in Zion. She's a woman very passionate and powerful concerning the things of God. What I have found in her as a leader is very rare. We appreciate you and we love you very much.

Of course, last but not least ... to my wonderful husband whom I adore, I thank you and I give you honor, not only for who you are in my life but for your full support during the writing of this book. You are my Boaz I am blessed to have you in my life. And I love you more than words can say.

INTRODUCTION

I can remember my experience battling the spirit of perversion and everything that I was going through;
I encountered all kinds of emotions and didn't really know what to do.
I knew what the Word said about ungodly
Lust, and as a believer of the gospel I knew what to do,
but as a wife ... I was at a loss.
My mistake was that I went into my marriage
looking for perfect love, which I've since learned one will never find
in the flesh. The only perfect love comes from God.
Then I realized there was nothing
else for me to do but be the me that God had
created me to be ... for Husband.
Today is the day for change and deliverance.

This book is to help all those who are affected by the spirit of perversion no matter what side of the fence you may be on whether you're male or female: for the saved and the unsaved, for those who are married or single, for those in ministry as well as for lay members. It's time for us to cry loud and spare not against this ungodly lust for the deliverance of God's people everywhere.

Being bound is no longer an option!

As a believer the end result of everything that we do should bring glory to God. And I have made my life transparent so that His glory can be magnified.

Table of Contents

Chapter One	Strength of a Stronghold	11
ChapterTwo	Admittance, Not Acceptance	21
Chapter Thee	Bruised	31
Chapter Four	Help 'em While You're Hurting	39
Chapter Five	The Lost Art	51
Chapter Six	Why My House?	61
Chapter Seven	The Naked Truth	71
Chapter Eight	The Weight of Forgiveness	83
Chapter Nine	When the Lights Go Out	93
Chapter Ten	Healing for Your Soul	101
Chapter Eleven	Not a "G" Thang	109
Powerful Reads and Materials:		121

CHAPTER ONE

Strength of a Stronghold

Before deliverance can take place one must come to the realization that he or she is bound by an evil or ungodly spirit. It also needs to be understood what being **bound** is, and what being **delivered** is and what they both consist of. **Bondage** can be defined as subjection to some force, compulsion, or influence. **Deliverance** is defined as "a setting free; a rescue or a release." And to **deliver** is defined as "to save from evil, danger, restraint; to liberate from bondage; to give forth; to transfer over."

So there fore it is safe to say that there is no need for deliverance if bondage is not present, just as there's no need for courage if fear is not present. But before we delve into this topic any further, a very important question must be asked and answered by whoever is bound, because without having this question answered none of this will be effectual: And that is...

Are you ready to be totally set free?

This is a question only the bound person can answer before the deliverance process can begin. Truth be told, regardless of how everyone surrounding the bound-up person may feel, nobody can make a person be delivered and set free; they have to want it for themselves. If someone is bound by vile lust, for instance, and if they acknowledge this bondage and freedom is desired, then God can do His work in that person's life like only He can. Now, after acknowledging this ungodly spirit, one must be willing to renounce perversion and all the powers that be, in full awareness that this may be easier said that done. First off; old Habits are hard to break because they are formed and fed over many years of time. They are practiced for such long periods that they become almost like a second nature for some people, and that is why they are so hard to break. In addition, spirits don't give up easily, especially if they have built a home in one's vessel. In fact, habits are conformed to such a natural activity that more times than none you can be indulging in an accustomed practice and not even recognize you're trapped in that bad habit until you've been into it for a short period of time. Realize this: Because habits become second nature, it's easy to be fooled into thinking they are just something you do; it's not as easy as people may think it is to break a bad habit because it has now formed into such a natural behavior, almost like a person who sucks his or her thumb. Have you ever known someone who sucked their thumb?

To everyone around them it's viewed as being nasty, something undesired, something the other person cannot comprehend doing. But the person who sucks their thumb can't see why everyone else gets so worked up about it, because the thumb-sucker actually sees it as harmless since it's not bothering anybody.

Or imagine if someone came to you and said that you could no longer take a bath. You've been bathing for so long that that statement would sound foreign to you. Though you can hardly compare the two that's how it is with a person who is bound by perversion; they see it as harmless. They feel that they're not hurting anybody, so what's all the fuss about? Not realizing that they are in fact hurting someone…**themselves (and if they are married their spouse).** And this is exactly what the enemy wants them/you to feel. This is referred to as a spirit of *delusion*, but we come against it today in the name of Jesus. One of my biggest problems during my battle with this spirit was that I couldn't understand *how* this could happen to us since we were saved and knew the Word of God. To me it was totally mind boggling how a person who knew the Word could do something against the Word, but we **all** do something against the Word of God everyday. May it be spoken, or in thought. Maybe what we do is not of this magnitude, but anything we do against the will of God is sin. The Word says there is no big sin or little sin; it's all sin in the eyes of God.

While in the deliverance process, God began to reveal some things to me concerning the spirit of perversion that not only helped me in my marriage but tools to also help others in the same fight. To help us come out victorious without being bitter.

According to the Hebrew translation, *Aplesis* denotes a release from bondage or imprisonment, and the corresponding verb is *Aphiemi*, which means to send away or to let go.

Jesus paid a price for release, which is translated in Greek as *Lutron*; the particular meaning of this word is a release that is affected **by payment of ransom.** This price was paid so that all individuals who are bound can be released. He's done His part; now we must do ours.

> *We know that our old self was nailed to the cross with him in order*
> *That our body which is the instrument of sin might be ineffective*
> *And inactive for evil, that we might no longer be slaves of sin*
> *(Romans 6:6 Amplified Bible).*

Some people's bondage came by way of generational curses, while others were ignited by way of introduction, such as something seen that aroused the psyche or something tasted and/or touched. We will visit these different aspects later. But even the smallest sin has the ability to grow into a stronghold, and be accompanied with a measure of heaviness, as that sin is fed continually. It is at this point when the one in bondage to the sin accumulates a strong satisfying gratification when they begin to indulge with pleasure in a corrupt affection that becomes habitual and uncontrollable.

These wayward lusts are embarrassing, they destroy families, and they claim households, but the hunger to indulge is forceful despite the many consequences it brings. There are some who have become so addicted and dependant on this gratification that they don't want deliverance on any level. Although all sins were initially activated in the Garden of Eden with Adam and Eve, sexual perversion wasn't mentioned in detail in the Old Testament until the Israelites came into the land of Canaan. The Lord had promised the Israelites (God's chosen people) the land of Canaan and He forbade them from adopting the vile lusts and practices of the Canaanites. (Read *Leviticus chapter 18,* which tells what God, thinks about unlawful sexual relations.)

Two of the hardest temptations to fight in the flesh are **the love of money** and **sexual immorality**. The struggle that many people have with these temptations is evident in everyday life. Take the media, for example; almost everything on the television, radio, and most literature is based on or derived from one or the two, with attention specifically focusing on two aspects:

1) Either how others are doing it, or
2) How you can get more of it.

There's an old cliché often mentioned in today's society, and humanity has adopted the mindset behind it: that "sex sells," and we have become willing victims to this concept, even to downright giving it away (let alone selling it).

Sex and sexual intercourse are *two* totally different acts.

According to Webster's dictionary...

Sex is defined as - either of two divisions; male or female, into which persons, animals, or plants are divided, or the characteristics of being either male or female.

So the word "sex" denotes *gender*.

Sexual Intercourse is defined as the "joining of the sexual organs" of a male and a female human being.

Subsequently, any such practice outside of marriage is ungodly; it is **sin**. Sexual gratification should only be between human flesh, male and female, husband and wife, the way God ordained it to be; that leaves homosexuality, pornography, and masturbation out of the box. Perversion is contentious because it goes against the laws of God. In opposition the enemy has managed to corrupt sexual gratification outside the guidelines that God put in order; that's just the way the enemy works. His profession is to do everything opposite to God and God's will, or to undo everything God has done, *all while trying to emulate God.* And when we accept a persons practices who indulges in these activities, we are embracing these distorted practices by default. My pastor once said in a Sunday morning service that the day is coming when **those of us who are not sexually immoral will become the minority.** God told Adam and Eve in the Garden of Eden to be fruitful and multiply; this was not just by way of cropping and harvesting but in childbearing as well. Looking at pornography (videos, magazines, TV, Internet, pictures, etc.) and the act of **masturbation** (which is the same thing as **a man's abortion**) eliminates the possibility of the reproduction of life and thus takes away the possibility of producing more sons of God in the earth.

Although this book deals with sexual perversion (in Christian marriages), perversion has many different faces. In my research I have found that there are more than one hundred recognized acts of perversion or paraphilia worldwide. But I'll just list a few of the more common practices...

Homosexuality - this is having sexual desire for someone of your same sex (gender)

Tri-sexuality - refers to those who will try anything once (not an official term)

Fornication - sexual intercourse between unmarried persons

Adultery - sexual relations between a married person and another person who is not their spouse

Ménage' trios or **Orgies** - sexual activity between two or more persons at the same time

Bestiality - engaging in malicious sexual acts with animals

Prostitution - the offer of sexual relations of any kind with agreement for payment by either drugs or money

Incest - sexual intercourse with family members

Dominatrix - someone who engages in sexual acts by way of seduction, to rule or control by superior power (this term usually refers to a female)

Pedophilia - an abnormal condition when an adult has sexual desire for children

Polygamy - having two or more spouses at the same time

Stripper or stripping - to gyrate or entertain in a provocative manner for entertainment purposes by the removal of clothing (piece by piece) for a possible exchange of payment

Rape or **Sexual Assault** - is the crime of having intercourse with a person by force and without consent

Peeping Toms - to look slyly; to secretly stare at the nakedness of another person without their foreknowledge or consent (commonly done by a male)

Sodomy - having sexual intercourse considered to be abnormal or in an abnormal way (anally or by mouth)

Phone sex / "900" numbers - sexually vulgar conversation, between persons via telephone for sexual gratification which usually includes groans and the act of masturbation

S & M or **Sexual Masochism** - indulging in savage beatings including harsh sexual behavior.

Molestation - touching, fondling, or having sexual physical contact with a minor.

Fetishism - when a nonsexual object excites or stimulates erotic feelings and emotions.

Though not listed specifically by name there are many scriptures that clearly detail how all these perversions go against God's law. Every one of these acts can destroy, ruin, and break a marriage, devastate a spouse not to mention damage your relationship with the Father. No one is exempt from being tempted to dabble in one or more of these perversions, and there aren't any excuses for anyone to do so, especially not for those in the body of Christ who claim the cross.

Please don't be tricked into thinking that the enemy has limited devices in misleading and distorting the hearts and minds of people everywhere. He has all kinds of wicked practices and behaviors, and surprisingly, many of these are committed in the beds of marriages between Christian husbands and wives, and I will be speaking on this later in the book.

There are individuals who are either **battling with** or **indulging in** these types of habits every day. In certain sectors of society and according to some beliefs, these vulgar passions are a part of ritualistic religious activity and cultural traditions. But let's read what the Bible says about that:

My people are destroyed for the lack of knowledge (Hosea 4:6 Amplified Bible).

That verse is speaking of the knowledge of God's Word (against these practices). But today we are coming against all these things that you or your spouse may be facing and/or struggling with so that the freedom Jesus already paid for with His death can be yours.

I decree and declare that today is your day of new beginnings by the cleansing of your heart and the renewing of you mind. In the name of Jesus, Amen.

CHAPTER TWO

Admittance, Not Acceptance

There are different steps and stages you must go through to get to deliverance; specifically, these steps must be taken in order to reach *total* deliverance.

Here are those key steps...

1) **Show admittance for your sin, not acceptance of it.** You must come to the full acknowledgment that you have been afflicted by a stronghold. You must make up in your mind that you want and need to be totally free. You must come to the realization that deliverance is a process, just like healing, and accept the possibility of relapse (for some people this is inevitable). But just like a child learning to ride a bike; in the event that you fall off, pick yourself up, dust yourself off and try again.

2) **Realize your need for repentance and forgiveness**.

Repentance is the main prerequisite for being forgiven of your sins by God. If you can admit something, then you can come to forgiveness for it. You serve a God who is ready and willing to forgive you. But you have to be able to go to God in all truth, and you might as well ... because **He already knows**. Even though He knows everything about you, He wants you to talk to Him in all honesty and sincerity so that He knows He has your heart. After getting right with God, forgive yourself, then there is the need of repentance and forgiveness that *must* be done between you and your spouse from one to another (if in fact you are married).

3) **Change your behavior**.

This is where integrity, morality, and nobility steps in. The way you think and act must change and fall into alignment with the word of God. You must put aside old habits for a new mindset. The enemy is known for attacking us in our thoughts and emotions. At this point you must ask the Lord to renew your heart and mind.

Though deliverance can happen overnight (because God *is* able to do so), most deliverance happens over a period of time, and this time span depends on the willingness and fight within you. It can happen sooner rather than later, but you have to keep the desire to be free. After you have acknowledged the spirit of perversion, you must renounce it before the process can begin. Another person *cannot* by any means make someone else want to be delivered; it only comes by the conviction of the Holy Spirit and the preached of the Word of God. Deliverance is something you have to want.

And if you truly don't want to be delivered but know you need to be, ask God to give you the heart and mind to want to be delivered.

4) You must renounce and denounce the spirit of perversion.

The word describes us as being " born in sin and shaped in iniquity;" thus, having the ability to commit sin comes very easily to us because we were born as sinners with a free will to choose either sin and death or redemption and salvation. But just because we were conceived as sinners we don't have to accept that as our destiny. That's why God is God; if we didn't need Him then we could have died and saved ourselves. Even a man being freed from a natural prison has a process he must go through before he is actually outside those prison walls and free to be a part of society again. We declare freedom for you through faith, and we trust God for total healing, but there is something that *you* must do. "Faith without works is dead;" believing to be free is just part of the process.

Another vital step on the road of deliverance is...

5) **Don't only pray at your weak moments; pray at your strong ones too.**
It is necessary to pray even when you're feeling strong so that when a weak moment does arise, God can keep you safe in the midst of it. Pray without ceasing concerning this thing; yes even when you don't think you need it. Store your prayers in heaven. Storing prayers literally saved my life. Know this, just because you make your mind up to be delivered does not mean that the enemy is going to just leave you alone. Temptations will continue to plague us until Jesus returns. You must push and fight to stay free at the same time, because if you stop you'll find yourself repenting for the same thing over and over again.

Although moving forward can be hard (harder than you thought it would be), just remember that moving backwards can cost you your inheritance and even your life, because the wages of sin is death.

6) **You must be willing to do whatever it takes to maintain your deliverance.**
You may be given advice such as, "Stay away from certain things on TV, don't go on the computer, walk away from the magazines," which are all things that may or may not help. But what about those imaginations that comes within your mind? Unlike magazines and television you can't just walk away from your mind. So, what then?

Suggestion: tell God what you're feeling right at that weak moment and ask Him to remove the thought. Begin to renounce the devil and resist it. The Bible says that if you resist temptation it will flee from you. Read the Bible until your mind has been cleansed by the Word, and then make yourself busy. Move from whatever spot you are in and begin to occupy yourself with doing something time-consuming and productive. For example, go clean the kitchen with your favorite gospel CD playing in the background. Start some laundry or go run a much-needed errand. The worst thing you can do in a weak moment is to just sit idle entertaining vulgar thoughts, letting the enemy have his way with your mind.

Also, while going through deliverance you must be willing to stay away from what has gotten you bound in the first place and from whoever has helped you indulge. Not revisiting these places is absolutely vital to your freedom. The enemy can always try and conjure up old temptations. If you feel the slightest inclination of excitement for ungodly sexual gratification, then most likely this is still a weakness for you, which means there is still a battle that needs to be won in that area of your life. Because you have served the devil through your sins in the past, trust me when I tell you — he knows what it is that tempts you, and he has plenty of whatever it is waiting with your name on it.

Remember what Jesus said in *Luke 11:24-26:*

When an unclean spirit is gone out of a man, he walketh through dry places, seeking rest; and finding none, he saith, I will return unto my house whence I came out. And when cometh, he findeth it swept and garnished. And when he cometh, he taketh to him seven other spirits more wicked than himself; and they enter in, and dwell there: and the last state of that man is worse than the first.

Beware of this happening to you. Don't just sweep and garnish your house, but furnish it with the Word of God. I once heard a preacher say **"abstinence is not deliverance."**

7) Put yourself in total submission to God and His Word.

Sometimes what God tells us to do isn't always easily done. He may tell you to give up some things temporarily, or He may tell you to stay away from some things permanently. And when it's something that has brought your flesh ungodly satisfaction, this process is much easier said than done. Admittance, not acceptance, says, "Yes, I have a problem, but I refuse to allow this thing to overtake or rule me." The devil is the father of lies, and we must not fall into league with what he says about us. God always has the final say in everything that concerns His children.

> *What therefore God hath joined together, let not man put asunder (Matthew 19:6).*

Not even Satan himself can tear apart what God has put together. Although this scripture talks about marriage and divorce, let's look at it from another aspect. There are certain things that we are waiting on God to do, but He's waiting on us to do them for ourselves. God is not going to do everything for us, simply because we are His children He gave us power to handle some things on our own. Think of how good parents raise their children. My parents did not always do everything for me, and it's a good thing they didn't, because imagine if they had; what would I have learned in life? How would I know how to make it on my own? Even if it means making mistakes every now and again, we've got to learn to put our God-given **power into action**. The spirit of perversion does not have to be accepted by either spouse, and both have the power to stand against it as long as they both have the Holy Spirit.

8) Know your weapons of warfare and use them wisely.

Sometimes we can lose a good fight simply by using the wrong weaponry. Or, we can put it like this: *"you can't bring a knife to a gun fight."*

What are the weapons of your warfare? Here are some to apply...

Perseverance and determination (having a made-up mind)

Fasting

Renouncing and denouncing all ungodly spirits

Prayer and supplications in the Spirit

Decreeing and declaring Gods Word

Reciting the Word and putting it into action

Speak the Word **boldly**

Faith with Works (because one without the other is ineffective)

Worship

Consecration

There is a method to binding and rebuking the enemy which is very effectual. And that method is...

1) Bind him – *to constrain him from running rampant*
2) Rebuke him – *to reprimand him through our authority*
3) Apply the blood – *to put Gods covering into operation*
4) Speak the Word – *verbalize what God says in opposition to what he says*
5) Cast him into dry places – *propel him into lifeless dwellings*

Putting on the whole armor of God is also key here (read *Ephesians 6:11-19*)

Here, defense and offense must work together. You confuse the enemy when he doesn't know your next move. When he thinks he has got you backed into the corner and you come from the other side of the room swinging, he's baffled because you caught him by surprise. And this is how we have to play it here. Not that this is a game, but what I'm trying to say is that you don't have to succumb to this spirit and its behavior and just blindly accept that this is the way it is. It doesn't *have* to be this way. There is another way to live and only **one** way out, and that's through Christ Jesus.

Water represents the Holy Spirit, right? There's a huge difference between **still** water and **stagnant** water. Mosquitoes and flies only fester around stagnant water, because that's where dead things live. *Stagnant* water is there, but nothing is moving. *Still* water is peaceful and tranquil. It sways gently, and there's a steady motion to its rippling, but deep beneath the quiet stream there are active signs of life. It's time to get moving yet **learn how to be still without being stagnant.** Learn how to activate your power against the enemy. Acceptance is not your reality, admittance is, and once this has been done deliverance is closer to you than before. This is the place where you develop a closer, more intimate relationship with the Father. When you first met your spouse and found that you could tell them anything, didn't that ignite a deeper affection in your heart for that person? That's what confession does for you, even when it's between you and the Father. It brings you closer to Him.

CHAPTER THREE

Bruised

*W*hat's wrong with me? You may be asking yourself this question continually on a daily basis. Dealing with the spirit of perversion may produce feelings of not being good enough, attractive enough, or desirable enough for your mate. Self-doubt has probably become a familiar place you visit in your mind several times a day. You are probably always comparing yourself to other people whom you think your mate may or may not be attracted to.

Am I too fat? Am I too skinny? Or maybe I'm not tall enough. This state of mind can haunt you repeatedly throughout a single day. But beware; pay attention to these thoughts, because even though you might have a justifiable reason for feeling the way you feel, this sort of mindset is dangerous on two levels:

One:

This attitude initiates feelings of depression, inferiority, insecurity, low self esteem, and an awful sense of self worth, just to name a few. All of these mindsets are the playing fields of the enemy.

Two:

Vulnerability is an open door for spirits of suicide, adultery, drug use or abuse, jealousy, and spirits of rejection to come in and invade your life.

Society has declared that feelings of depression, oppression, and suppression are serious mental illnesses for which doctors and psychiatrists all over this continent prescribe medication, calling it chemical imbalances in the brain, and medically this may be a fact. But spiritually these are nothing more than heavy spirits that have the ability to paralyze people's emotions. We have to fight these spirits mentally and with the Word of God before they try to overtake our mind and cause us to believe what the enemy says we are; we must focus on who God says we are. Let's take a quick look at Scripture to prove my point.

According to *Genesis chapter three*, everything that God created in the Garden of Eden He gave to Adam and his wife Eve to nurture and have dominion over.

They were instructed to do this task together ... as a team, which means they were to be with one accord, which implicates that they were to build a dwelling place together. In other words, if one had the seeds, the other was to water. Or if I buy the popcorn then you buy the drink. But something happened in Eve that didn't happen in Adam. Out of all that God had given them, the enemy was able to put Eve's sights on the *one* thing that she could not have. Isn't that just like the enemy ... trying to make us think and feel that God is an unjust God?

> *But God said, you shall not eat of the fruit of the tree which is in the midst of the garden, neither shall you Touch it, lest you die. But the serpent said to the woman, you will not die. For God knows that when you eat of it your eyes will be opened and you will be like God, knowing good and evil (Genesis 3:3-5).*

Because Eve's mind was an open playing field, the enemy was able to cause her feelings toward God to be amiss, which was the tool that was used to shift mankind from its original relationship with God to being sinful creatures apart from God. This is serious stuff, isn't it? And the enemy has not changed his methods; he is still using this very same tactic today in everyday life and in marriages all over the world. Out of everything that God has blessed us with, the enemy takes our vulnerability and desires and uses those weaknesses for his gain. If we allow him to, he'll put our focus on the *one* thing we don't have, and we'll make that our primary focus. And some of us step out from under the sheltering umbrella of God to pursue that *one* thing we so desire. I have seen this happen to some of the most anointed men and women of God in the church.

I've seen people leave God for money, cars, fame and success, **new mates/spouses** (which is a common one), houses, and children ... all because the enemy was able to make them think differently about the perfect timing of God and His promises for their lives.

The enemy is not indifferent. Allow me to explain something; you can own a five bedroom house, be an executive of the biggest company in this country, own a Maybach automobile, have an indoor pool, and have a cottage on the beach of Hawaii, but if your mind is not in tune with the peace of God, you can lose your focus, and then with the enemy's help you will shatter your already stressed marriage. In *Ephesians 6:11*, the Bible talks about the girding of your mind and the importance of putting on the whole armor of God.

You are beautifully and wonderfully made. And although you may be hurting and struggling with the feeling of insecurity, God is a healer of hearts and minds. I know firsthand what you may be feeling right now, and as hard as it is to believe ... it does get better if you allow the Lord to heal you.

I can remember when my husband and I were in the midst of our fight against the spirit of perversion; I began to have feelings of insecurity, not in my marriage but in myself as a person. I began comparing myself to women on TV and women on magazine covers, which now seems so foolish. But at the time it didn't seem foolish at all; if felt logical to try to become what I thought he was attracted to. I did this because I love him and I wanted to please him. I didn't take time to realize that I already was the woman he was attracted to when he chose to marry me, **and there was nothing else for me to do but be the me whom God had created for him**. I noticed the spirit of low self esteem trying to creep in slowly and I began to feel myself falling into the spirit of low feelings. The enemy saw that as an open door and tried to use that to his advantage. But I had to fight in my mind and denounce the spirit of low self esteem before it turned into a spirit of depression, or even worse. If I had allowed it to overtake me it could have drove me into the arms of another man (who liked thick girls, because they are "out there") all in the name of looking for affirmation. I knew that and so did the enemy, and he would have had one of those men waiting in the cut, who would have been more than willing to help me fall and destroy my marriage, so that the enemy could laugh in my face.

Because of low self esteem and not knowing how to deal with what I was feeling. I could have allowed the enemy to occupy my mind with all kinds of ungodly thoughts. This is how the devil works. Adultery only makes bad things worse, and trust me; my marriage would have eventually ended in divorce. I would have been added to the statistic that fifty percent of all Christian marriages fail.

Understand something: I wasn't contemplating an affair I loved my husband; (and still do) with all my heart, but when a feeling of rejection takes hold of you, you begin to look for affirmation and attention wherever you can find it. That's why you find some people jumping in relationship after relationship.

It wasn't that I had a bad marriage, or an abusive husband, but rather, my mistake was that I went into this marriage expecting perfect love, which you will never find in the flesh. This is the kind of love that says, "I will never hurt you." Has anybody ever said that sweetly to you? Can I get anybody to be honest? We've probably said it to someone a time or two ourselves, only to then do or say something that hurts them. I heard that plenty of times long before my husband. But God had to let me know that the only perfect love comes from Him. I knew that I was my husbands' helpmeet, but I just didn't know how to help bring him to his full potential in God, wear the smile, and fight this thing all at the same time. But I gave God a chance to work on my marriage. Sometime we act **too** quickly out of emotion and we don't give God the chance to fix everything in His time. My dad always says, "Never make a decision when you're emotional."

If you are the spouse of someone who is tempted by sexual sin, one thing you must realize is it has absolutely nothing to do with you. If your mate was married to Halle Berry, LL Cool J, or the most famous porn star in the world, they would still struggle with this same spirit of perversion.

Please know that they are not drawn to sexual sin because **you** are unattractive or undesirable. Perversion could not care less about who they are married to or how you feel or about the call on your mate's life. It has no respect of persons and is not by any means indifferent. Its purpose is to pollute, tear down, break up, and ruin your marriage ... not to mention, to pull you away from God. You say that you can't make it, and you say that it's too strenuous, but I say to you, yes, you can make it! I made it through and so can you by the grace of God.

Be strong in the Lord and in the power of his might (Ephesians 6:10).

You were chosen by your mate for what he or she saw in you and liked because it defined who you are, so why compare yourself to others now? Don't allow the enemy to make you believe that you have to look or be like somebody else to get your mate to desire you. Have you ever watched one of these popular television shows where people get complete makeovers almost to the point of looking like another human being? That is a direct insult to God as our Creator. By re-doing themselves they're indirectly saying, "God, you didn't do a good job when you created me, and I can do better."- None of us has bodies that stay the very same as they were when we were courting and then were young newlyweds. So I'm not talking about the changes of life, those natural changes that come with age and maturity that might be slightly improved with a little help. I'm referring to those total body makeovers done with the intent to look like someone else in order to get your mate to long for you.

Beauty is in the eye of the beholder, and that must first start with you.

CHAPTER FOUR

Help 'em While You're Hurting

Dealing with the spirit of perversion (in your spouse) can feel like you're caught in the middle of a powerful hurricane, and just like with a hurricane, the onslaught can hit you on many different levels. The damage perversion causes can be anywhere from *minimal damage* to *catastrophic,* and the only safe place to be is in the eye of the storm where everything is calm. No matter the damage, and no matter what sort of catastrophic storm you're going through in your marriage, you can rest in the Lord. He *is* the eye of the storm.

If you're the nonoffending spouse in this dilemma, it will be difficult to understand the desire or the actions of your spouse, who's in bondage yielding to that wayward lust, but that does not take away the requirement of your presence and support; they need you desperately. Your job is not to try and understand this uncontrollable desire but instead to just be strong enough in the spirit of the Lord to stand against it. By understanding the desire, you may fall subject to the same spirit.

Your job is not to condemn but to lift your mate up in continual prayer before the Lord.

When the final moment came for me to make a decision as a wife concerning my marriage, there were several things I could have done: I had the choice to get a divorce, look the other way, or confront the issue and get it resolved together as husband and wife.

Being in love with him and wanting to keep my marriage vow, I decided divorce wasn't an option for me. Looking the other way wasn't going to work either because of my passion for ministry, and not only for my ministry but his as well. So the only other option was to confront the issue head on. And when I say confront I'm talking about doing so on two different levels: coming to terms with what needed to be fought — and confronting the evil spirit that was trying to destroy my marriage and our ministry.

Embarrassment was inevitable. I wondered how people were going to view me as his wife. I felt the fear of all the backlash and ridicule from out side people. I wondered what family and friends would have to say. And I worried how people were going to react to him as a man of God. Seeing how the church world is under a microscope now wasn't a popular time to go public with our story. But after contemplating what I should do, I realized there was no time for me to have an embarrassed mindset because not only was I hurting, but he was too. And like us there are many dealing with the same issue. My pastor once said" although the Jeremiahs prophesies were not popular, doesn't mean they weren't of God". In this book you'll hear me repeat "As children of God we have to adopt the mind set of; the end results of everything that we do should be glory to God". *So I have made my life transparent so that His glory can be magnified.* I had to take myself out of the box and think about all the me's out there. I had to remove my feelings from the equation and understand how he felt as a minister of the gospel. And when I realized that, instead of being embarrassed I became *very* proud of my marriage and my husband, and to this day I've *never* looked at him the same. This is our testimony and this testimony can be yours. God can do it.

My support was needed as a wife, as a helpmeet, and as a friend, more than ever. I decided that if people were going to talk, then they were just going to have to talk about both of us, because I wasn't going to let us go down without a fight. If everyone else was going to point the finger, the last person expected to assist in the ridicule was one of the person I thought was hurting the most ... **me**. We needed each other as a support system, and this was the biggest test of our marriage thus far. My spiritual father is a Pastor, so we naturally chose him to officiate at our wedding. I can still remember him reading this scripture during the ceremony:

> *Above all, love each other deeply, because love covers over a multitude of sins*

(1 Peter 4:8). God knew we would have to face this problem ... and God also knew that He had called us to the ministry, so He had to give my husband someone (me) who wasn't going to run away out of fear and embarrassment, but someone who would fight through the struggle, all the way to deliverance. Marriage if full of tests and trials, and one of the hardest tests is when you've got to be a good spouse when you're marriage is being tested. Sometimes it seems easier to run or look the other way, but we have to keep the mindset of God getting the glory out of every situation. This is the place where you both need healing from the same spirit but on two different levels, and God has the power to do both. Some storms are unexpected, but there are those storms that send warning signs before they hit. My worst catastrophe may not be your worst, and your worst may not be mine. Everyone's storm comes with different effects, but how you withstand the storm will determine what goods are salvaged after the worst has passed.

You may be thinking *what else can I do? I'm mentally and emotionally tired and it's not getting any better.* But it does get better. After you've done all you can do, move aside and allow God to do all He can do. Your battles are not yours to fight alone. This is the time to put your spiritual warfare into action. The outcome depends not only on your skill level and ability to fight, but on how much you let God fight your battles with you.

I found myself helping him while I was hurting at the same time. I had to remind myself of this scripture:

> *If a man be overtaken in a fault, ye which are spiritual,* **restore such an one in the spirit of meekness;** *considering thyself, lest thou also be tempted.* **Bear ye one another's burdens,** *and so fulfill the law of Christ (Galatians 6:1-2).*

Some of you are at a place where your mate has actually come to you and extended the invitation for you to indulge in some of these perverse activities right along with them. A lady that I had the opportunity to speak with said that her spouse has now asked her to watch pornography with him, insinuating that it'll spice up their love life. At first he was watching these movies by himself, but now he's invited her to the party. In tears she said to me, "I know it's wrong, and it makes me feel so uncomfortable; I know God is watching me, but I love my husband, so what else can I do?"

Against popular opinion I said, "Take a stand for holiness and say *No.*" I told her, "Explain to him that it makes you feel uncomfortable and how the conviction of the Lord is weighing heavy on your heart. His love for you should never want to put you in a compromising position.

Misery loves company and so does sin. Are you in this place? I know the hardness of a situation like this. I myself haven't experienced it firsthand, but I can imagine the heartache this can bring to a spouse that really wants to live a Christian lifestyle. If this describes what you're also facing, know this: someone has to take a stand for what is right. **No matter how the world changes, holiness is still right!** If you want your mate to be delivered, then committing sin along with him or her is not the answer. Indulging in these wrong practices with them is not helping the situation. It's making matters worse, because now *both* of you are caught up and not just one.

I know that there are a lot of Christian married couples who watch pornography together, but doing so is a sin because it is uncovering someone else's flesh. The Word of God speaks against this. If you really take a good look at this situation this is nothing more than a big orgy between you and another couple (that you do not know). You need to figure out - what it is about watching other people having sex that turns you on. You need to check the spirit behind that urge. That perverse spirit comes right out of the TV and straight into you and that spirit has connected itself with yours that is why it has the ability to ignite feelings in you because now that spirit has been transmitted. This is not godly. I love my husband very much, so why would I need to watch another man having sex with another woman to make me stirred? If this describes you, then you are being tricked.

This is not okay. You may be thinking that because you're married you are in a safe zone, when actually you are in a danger zone. **Marriage does not make this permissible.** It is still indulging in pornography, and if one person watching it alone is considered perversity, then how is it alright just because two married people are watching it together? You're still watching pornography no matter how much you justify it.

If your spouse is battling the spirit of perversion, know that you are not alone in this. Depending on your level of determination you can "beat the beast." During the writing of this book I had the opportunity to interview four different people who were married four out of the four are in the church sector just to find out their take on the spirit of perversion in Christian marriages. To my surprise, out of the four people I spoke with, **all** four was dealing with the spirit of perversion in the household on one level or another. This problem is more common than some may want you to believe. It isn't talked about enough because of shame, quilt, and embarrassment. One of the people I spoke with admitted they are even embarrassed to tell people that they are Christians because of their spouse's behavior. And this is common also.

One lady said that because she refused to do certain acts that her husband wanted to try because of what he had seen in a porn film, she knew he was on his way to actually committing adultery. This downhill slide in their marriage began with him wanting her to watch porn movies with him. And this is how many Christians get sucked into sin.

She expressed to me the uneasiness she feels every time she watches the movies with him. But to please her husband and keep him from watching them with someone else, she gives in. In tears she asked me, "What do I do?"

I told her, first you need to repent for your participation in it, then you need to "Call that spirit by name and rebuke it out of your home and your spouse. It's time for you to go into spiritual warfare, turn your plate down, and beat that chief before it destroys your marriage." There is **nothing** too hard for God. And he's trying (the enemy) to steal our ministries, and marriages right from under our noses. One key thing to understand about this weakness is something that my husband shared with me: the gratification one gets is only temporary.

When he told me that I finally realized why it gets so extreme for some people — because they're constantly looking for the ultimate gratification, and once they reach one level of gratification, they seek out the next level.

It's almost like a drug; once your body gets used to one drug, you look for a stronger drug that will take you a little higher than the previous one. That's why sexual perversion usually starts off with magazines, then it progresses to watching XXX-rated movies, then to convincing someone else to watch the porn with them, and then to suggesting -

'let's try this together,'? Then to masturbation, and all sorts of ungodly activities follow after that.

Ask God for the wisdom on how to deal with the situation in *your* house, because every situation is not the same. Also, ask God to heal you while He's bringing deliverance to your mate. **Remember to stay in the eye of the storm ... the center of calm.** Your marriage is being tested right here, so fight right here! I know you feel tired and you don't know what else to do. Let go and let God. Allow Him to deal with your pain and take it away. *Every* storm is accompanied by rain. Just because it rains doesn't mean the sun will never shine again. Always remember, rain signifies *restoration and replenishment.*

A lot of people have been misguided into believing that God does not care about what takes place in our bedrooms during intimacy because we are married, but that is not true at all. The fact of the matter is that He does care. He cares so much about the intimacy of a true marriage relationship that He considers His own relationship with us (His church) to be a marriage. And when we become intimate with Him through our praise and worship, He dwells therein. Intercourse is *not* intimacy. Many people in the church world get offended when they hear someone say, "Come on, let's have intercourse with God." Have you ever heard something like that during a worship experience? If you have, it's important to understand that this is not the correct connotation of this word. It would be better to say, "Let's be intimate with God through our praise and worship."

Intimacy is defined as the state or fact of being intimate; intimate association; familiarity.

Intercourse is defined as communication or dealings between or among people; interchange of products, services, ideas, feelings, etc. (Although the word intercourse can also relate to sexual intercourse, in this definition I'm referring to just intercourse.)

The world today has become so modern that even our traditional marriage vows have changed on a dramatic level. For those of us who still choose to say the traditional vows, those vows included the phrase *"to have and to hold, for better or for worse."* Depending on the level of perversion you may be dealing with in your marriage, let me suggest something to you, and that is to **never allow anyone to dictate to you what your "worse" should be.** I think I need to say that twice....

"Never allow anyone to dictate to you what your "worse" should be."

Not for a second am I suggesting that you accept any kind of bad treatment, because there are some marriages that are dealing with far greater issues than the spirit of perversion. But what I am saying is that God instituted marriage; therefore He is for marriage, and if we are truly His children then we should love what He loves and hate what He hates. It is absolutely mind boggling to me how Christians are being told by other saints that they should leave their spouses over issues that God can work out.

There will be times in our marriages when we will be tested by our vows of commitment. Not every issue we face will be small enough to sweep under the rug without detection. If you lay a flat piece of paper under a rug, no one will be able to detect that it's hidden there, but if you took that same piece of paper and balled it up and placed it back under the same rug, it will instantly become obvious that something is underneath the rug that doesn't belong there, because the rug is no longer a decoration but a eye soar. **Some issues may require more effort and tears to fix than others**, but that doesn't mean they're impossible to fix. We're quick to quote, "God can do anything but fail," yet we only believe that to a certain degree.

Allow me to admonish you to let go and let God.

This is not your opportunity to point the finger or give your mate the door and tell him or her that they are on their own. Realize that their deliverance is what you want and have prayed for. Ask God to give your spouse the heart and mind to be delivered, if they don't have one right now. Never lose yourself in all of this; I knew that I needed healing from the effects of this perverse spirit, but I had to be willing to place myself on the lookout post *and* receive my own healing at the same time. It's kind of like spiritual multitasking!

CHAPTER FIVE

The Lost Art

There's an old saying that most of us learned in childhood: "Stick and stones may break my bones but words will never hurt me."

That is so far from the truth; what we say *does* hurt people, and the pain goes far deeper than we can imagine. What you say has the ability to kill a person's spirit, create or destroy a person's character, break up a home, catapult someone into greatness or keep them from ever achieving anything, and so on. Words are very powerful because they go into a person's soul. Despite popular belief, no matter how much you apologize to an individual, you can never take back the hurtful things you said to them no matter how hard you try ... it's impossible. The scripture says this…

> *Death and life are in the power of the tongue: and they that love it shall eat the fruit thereof (Proverbs 18:21).*

The bible also calls the tongue an unruly member. So, why are we so surprised when other people are wounded by the hurtful things that we say to them? Some people are so hurt they even go as far as leaving their church in an effort to make a fresh start, all because what they shared with someone privately was broadcast and made public knowledge or other similar situations (but all involving the tongue).

The reason I want to deal **intensely** with this subject is because a large number of people are really being damaged by something that seems so trivial – mere words, or so they say. Despite how you may feel about what you have done, God is saying, "You are hurting my children."

> *And the King shall answer and say unto them, Verily I say unto you, Inasmuch as ye have done it unto one of the least of these my brethren, ye have done it unto me*
>
> *(Matthew 25:40).*

In this scripture Jesus is saying that we should not hurt even the least ones of His children. In a little while I'll explain why I'm so desperately trying to drive home this point to every heart reading this book: that things shared in confidence must be kept private so that no one gets hurt.

We have to learn how to keep someone's intimate secrets private and treat those secrets like we do our own. And we must also come to realize how tender people can be with their personal lives.

Webster dictionary defines **confidence** as "trust, reliance, assurance; belief in one's ability to be trusted; the belief that another will keep a secret. Something told in secret."

We have to display ourselves as people of good class and quality. We have to make it a point to display finesse with people's private battles and affairs. Way too many people have been lost or have turned away from Christianity with bitterness in their hearts because of this. They are literally leaving their churches or, even worse, some are leaving God altogether ... *and at what cost?*

Taking on the "blood-stained banner of Christ" automatically comes with tests and trials, but some of this stuff is our fault and we can't get around it; that's a fact. Not all people are mentally strong enough to withstand the rumors, gossip, and the "he said and she said" trap. There are no more excuses for what we have done in the body of Christ by saying things like, "They should have known better" (once the wounded ones have left the church). Or some even say, "Well, maybe they weren't really saved anyway." But that's not our call to make, is it? That's God's call.

Confidentiality has become a *Lost Art* in our churches.

Our secret affairs haunt us to such an extent that people are now afraid to seek the proper deliverance that the King is offering. Most people come to church looking for God because they've tried everything else, or because they have issues that they can no longer handle on their own, and we're supposed to be God's advocates, walking in wisdom when we deal with the hurting, wounded folk. So why do we have so many people saying, "I'll never go back to that church"? What transpired in that particular church that helped increase the statistic of churches being filled with hypocrites to an all-time high?

Now please, don't get me wrong ... I'm not referring to the people who leave or backslide because their sin was not tolerated by leadership and they refused to repent. I honor leadership to the utmost and you should too. You should always respect those who have rule over you (no exceptions) and have full confidence in God's spirit within your leader. I'm not referring to godly management, guidance, or direction; I'm referring to the rumors, gossip, and hearsay that may or may not hold any truth.

Let's create a quick scenario: If Brother Bobby comes to you in confidence about anything that he's dealing with, (meaning, something that has simply been shared in confidence), then he has the right to expect his personal privacy will be respected by you. So before you spread the word ask yourself ... "If Brother Bobby found out that I told Brother Sammy what he shared with me in confidence, would it hurt him?" If your answer is "yes," then allow me to strongly suggest that you should not say a word to anyone about what Brother Bobby has shared with you. Not only is that called confidence that is also having a good Persona'.

The reason I'm dealing with confidence in a book discussing perversion is this...

Too many church people (God's children) are walking around battling with the spirit of perversion (as well as other things), and they prefer to battle with these things alone rather than go to someone in the church to seek help because of their fear of losing confidentiality or being the target of the gossip and the stares . God wants his people healed, set free, and delivered, but we have damaged so many people's trust in so many ways to the point where now we have a whole lot of saved, sanctified folk still bound and seeking out psychiatrists and doctors to help them with their issues. I'm not knocking the psychological or medical professions, but if a psychiatrist does not know God and does not live by the ordinances of God, how can he/she accurately (with godly wisdom) counsel a child of God? This is out of order.

And after all is said and done, these therapists are suggesting to these saints of God that it's natural to explore sexually with these ungodly lusts, and that they should take some to time to discover their bodies and their sexuality by indulging in these vile passions. The devil is a liar! And a lot of them are still bound in some instances we have done this to our people, not God.

Or ... you have a bunch of Christians going to group counseling and joining support groups seeking help amongst the ungodly, all while belonging to deliverance ministries. There are Christians consulting with social workers on how to manage the different matters of life. And as a result, they are still bound and are probably worse off than if they didn't seek worldly counsel, all because they're not getting the deliverance they need because of fear. I'm referring to the type of deliverance that only comes from God with the help of the brethren. How does this look for the body of Christ? Where is God's glory in that? The secular world is supposed to come to us for help, not the other way around. This is a backwards system, and we the believers must take the responsibility and the initiative to turn it back around.

Now do you understand my point? We have to love the people back to God and get rid of our own intents. This is bigger than our cliques and our little inner circle of friends and associates with whom we share everything we know. We are devastating the children of the King for our own personal enjoyment. Though this book is about the spirit of perversion, some of us need to get delivered from the spirit of talking too much. I can remember when it was finally time to come to terms with this spirit in my marriage; I was going through all kinds of emotions and didn't really know what to do. I knew what the Word said about ungodly lust. And

I knew what to do as a minister of the gospel, but as a wife I was at a loss, besides the fact that I was a new bride. So, not really knowing what I should do, I called my pastor. We were able to go to our leader with the full assurance that she had the wisdom of God to help us handle this issue as a couple. And with the love, wisdom, and patience of God displayed through her, my husband and I was able to get the deliverance and healing that we needed. She dealt with our situation as tenderly as could be, with compassion for our marriage accompanied with the strength of God's anointing so that she could come against that spirit. She was able to be gentle and strong at the same time. And when the time came for that spirit to be confessed and repented of publicly, she let my husband tell it to our brothers and sisters in Christ on his own accord. And with that; we were embraced by our whole body *as the couple that was victorious* and not the couple that's going through. I know that what we found in our pastor as a leader is **very** rare. But by being able to go to my shepherd in confidence and having that confidence kept, we were able to build a trust in her not only as a Pastor but as a mentor who walks in godly integrity. She is very passionate about people being delivered. So if and when the next issue arises in our marriage, we (my husband and I) know that our leader will counsel us with the wisdom of God and that it will not be posted in the church bulletin for all to read. This kind of godly leadership is what every church needs.

It's time for us to walk in nobility and compassion ... ***not for the sin, but for the souls***. Because if human beings can't trust us with their most intimate secrets, how can God? There are some things that the Lord would love to share with us, but He can't because we'll either tell it to the wrong person or tell it too prematurely, and we'll mess the whole thing up. As the Bible says, we must "study to be quiet."

> *Brothers, if someone is caught in a sin, you who are spiritual should restore him gently. But watch yourself, or you also may be tempted*
>
> *(Galatians 6:1).*

We must begin to place ourselves in position and get in alignment with the Word of God. It is imperative we that show forth the kindness and concern of God with empathy and with consideration for others. Isn't that's what *Galatians 6:1* is talking about? ... So that the hurting can find refuge in the house of God and not find a bunch of gossipers. No, not everyone that goes to church is saved, so you will have some folk who won't be convicted in their hearts about the sin of spreading rumors, but those of us who are filled with the Holy Ghost and are spiritually mature should know the crucial importance of protecting someone else's right to confidence. Another person's intimate secrets are not for our listening enjoyment. Indulging in someone else's set backs to tickle the ear. Church is a refuge and healing place but what have we turned it into?

Now there are some instances where certain things must be called out openly before the congregation, but that decision is up to **God** and **your leadership**. But God is a God of love, not embarrassment. And when He (God) decides to call something to the forefront before the people, it is either to deliver a person, save a persons life before they hit destruction, or for open rebuke about a sin that has hurt the entire church body, and even then this open rebuke should be done out of love, not for everyone else's listening pleasure. It's God's job to expose sin. And the last time I checked, no one that I know created the wind.

CHAPTER SIX

Why My House?

Those who are controlled by ungodly spirits of pornography and masturbation usually justify their activities with lies they tell themselves (and others) such as: "What's everybody tripping about?" ... "This is harmless" ... "I'm not hurting anybody" ... "Nobody else knows, so just chill out" ... or the all-time favorite, "This is not a problem; I can stop anytime I want." Don't be alarmed because they actually believe this stuff; this is what the enemy has told them, and although it's a recurring problem, they still believe they can stop whenever they want to.

Those who struggle with porn and masturbation become especially skilled at convincing themselves of these lies. They think that as long as there's no penetration between persons in the sex act then no sin has been committed, but let's see what Jesus says about this:

> *But I say to you that everyone who so much as looks at a woman with lust in his heart for her has already committed adultery with her in his heart (Matthew 5:28).*

According to Scripture the deed has been done. Until the person who is bound by this sin recognizes it as an ungodly stronghold, they will continue to justify their lustful practices. They will come up with all kinds of reasons why these vulgar affections are harmless, even though it goes against the Word of God and His ordinances.

Have you ever met the type of people in the church world who use scriptures to justify their wrongdoing? Maybe you've done this a time or two. I know I have. We all have at one point or another; let's keep it real. I know of an evangelist who is an undercover lesbian and is seriously struggling with the spirit of homosexuality. Those who know of her ungodly, undercover lifestyle have confronted her on this issue once or twice, and she always justifies it by saying, "Gifts and callings are without repentance." I'm not judging her gift of evangelism, but I tell this story to show you how the enemy has people tricked in their minds. It's a heavy spirit of *delusion*. Some people don't even want deliverance — they just don't want to be caught in their lust. **But God is a revealer**. I've heard some people say as an excuse, "Well, nobody knows what Paul's 'thorn in the flesh' was." Have you ever heard that one?

Let me sound the alarm on this type of justification.

Let's take a look at the scripture that such people are quoting from when they say "gifts and callings are without repentance," and then I will deal briefly with it in the context of what was going on at the time Paul wrote it:

> *For the gifts and calling of God are without repentance*
> *(Romans 11:29).*

Paul was referring to the fallen sons of Israel in this scripture. Israel was given a covenant because of their forefathers. Despite their disobedience and rebellion, they were still God's chosen people. Just because you have the gift doesn't mean you are not in a fallen state. This scripture was referring to *a fallen people* that God still loved, but that does not take away their sin.

What Paul *is* saying here is that God has given them mercy through their rebellious state. Mercy does not erase sin; it simply protects you while you're in sin.

In addition, let's deal with those who compare their sin with the Apostle Paul's thorn. *True!* No one knows exactly what his thorn was but how are we so bold as to place ourselves in the league with the great Apostle Paul. When we have suffered what he has suffered for the sake of the gospel then we can talk comparison.

Be careful! Be very careful as to how you use God's Word to cover your secret sins in an attempt to make God's people accept such lifestyles in the church. I'm not sending anyone to heaven or hell in this book. Clearly I don't have the authority to do that, but I do have the authority (and the responsibility) to share with you what the Word says about it; let's read how it speaks very authoritatively on this matter:

Many will say to me in that day, "Lord, Lord, have we not

> *Prophesied in thy name? And in thy name have cast out devils? And in thy name done many wonders works?"*
>
> *And then will I profess unto them, I never knew you: depart from me, ye that work iniquity (Matthew 7:22-23).*

No one can argue with that. We are not judges, but we ***are*** fruit inspectors. And there is a scripture that says, *"For the tree is known by his fruit" (Matthew 12:33)*. I have never seen an apple and an orange dangle from the same tree. But all can be healed by the power of God's Word.

I've learned that what is a weakness for one person may be someone else's strong point. A person struggling with an ungodly spirit should never seek help from a person with that same weakness that is also battling with the same spirit.

Although *the spirit is willing, the flesh is still weak (see Matthew 26:41)*. The Bible warns us how the devil desires to sift us like wheat.

People acquire spirits through many different ways. You may be wondering how a saved person can develop such ungodly affections. Some ways that ungodly spirits can come over a person are by way of experimentation, looking for love in ungodly relationships out of their loneliness, through carried-over spirits (spirits they had before getting saved), from being molested at a young age, from generational curses, from watching porn on TV or on the Internet, and surprisingly, some may even form ungodly behavior that was suggested to them by another church brethren (this one shocked me when I learned that it actually happens).

I knew a brother in the Lord who struggled with pornography and masturbation; when I say struggled, I mean ***really*** struggled. He had indulged in this activity since around the tender age of maybe eleven or twelve. He had been doing it for so long that he could no longer get pleasure from a woman; he preferred obtaining sexual gratification from himself. He would indulge in this activity about two or three times a day. He acknowledged that he had a problem when he realized how much he wanted to get married to a young lady in his church whom he'd been dating. He wanted to stop but he couldn't; the urge to indulge was just too strong. When he told his lady friend what he was battling with, she wanted to help him; with her caring heart she suggested that he go to see a doctor. He followed her advice, and the physician told him that he had done self-gratification for so long that his body no longer recognized a female as being sexually alluring, and thus he would have to literally retrain his thought patterns to once again have sexual desires for women and not for himself. This meant the masturbation had to stop completely, which for him was the hardest part. He agreed to stop watching the XXX-rated videos, but he didn't want to throw them away. He needed God to deliver him. One day I asked him, "How did this start with you? What triggered this ungodly desire?" And to my surprise he told me that when he was about eleven or twelve years old he began to feel his hormones kick in, and not having a father in his life to give him guidance he went to one of the deacons in his church to seek guidance with these new feelings he was struggling with. In his conversation he shared with the deacon what he was feeling and what his body was experiencing. The deacon told him that it was okay to have these feelings, that they were natural; they come with growing up, and that some brothers go through that early in life.

Okay, so this was good information, I thought as I listened. I was in agreement with the story until he told me that the deacon had told him that he (the deacon) would bring him a porno from home and give it to him to watch, and he suggested that he should masturbate while watching it. Then he said that the deacon told him **no sin was being**

committed since he wouldn't actually be penetrating a woman. I was floored.

Now I'm not saying that all people in the body of Christ are making these kinds of suggestions, but we need to be made aware of how some of this stuff is being brought into the churches, and then we need to take a thorough look of how many people we have in ministerial leadership positions battling with all kinds of vile lusts and not being delivered themselves.

One may question ... *Why my house? Why my family? Why my loved one? Why me?* But understand this, and I've said it before: spirits are not indifferent and could not care less about your plans for your life or your ideas for your family. Spirits will use and exploit any able, willing body that is dead to Christ or weak in the spirit. Such spirits feed off of spiritual weakness, those places in us that we don't nourish. Some spirits are easier to combat than others, and for those heavy battles you need heavy artillery. There are evil spirits that are chiefs and generals who dwell in the high places of the wicked. There's a saying that goes, "Just a dab'll do ya." But deliverance from some of these spirits calls for serious fasting and praying. (Re-read chapter two, **Admittance, not Acceptance**, and find out what your weapons of warfare and the methods to binding and rebuking the enemy.)

For we wrestle not against flesh and
Blood, but against principalities, against powers,

against the rulers of darkness of this world, against spiritual wickedness in high places (Ephesians 6:12).

When the disciples could not cast out the lunatic demon as described in *Matthew 17:13-21*, they asked Jesus, "Why couldn't we cast the spirit out?" He answered and said to them, **"This kind** *goeth not out but by prayer and fasting."* The words *this kind* tells us that they weren't dealing with a peek-a-boo baby spirit; they were dealing with a heavy psychopathic spirit. Those two words *this kind* indicate that they were dealing with a strong spirit that needed strong combat. When we look at *verse 16* we read that the disciples were trying to "cure" him and nothing happened. But Jesus spoke to that spirit with authority and power.

Let's take a look at *verses 16 and 18* to compare the difference between the disciples' efforts and what Jesus was able to accomplish:

I brought him to your disciples, but they could not heal him ... Jesus rebuked the demon, and it came out of the boy, and he was healed from that moment.

Jesus knew that this spirit called for the heavy artillery. Through the Holy Spirit that dwells within you, you've got to speak to that spirit and stop wasting time nagging at the flesh. Nagging wouldn't have done any good; all that would have done is frustrated the situation, him, and myself. But once we began to rebuke the evil spirit and speak God's Word to that spirit, we began to see change. Remember what I said about asking God to give your mate a mindset of wanting to be free. Once this happens they will be able to admit they have a problem and want to be set free. This book is not about *who* was struggling in my home opposed to what I have learned, how I want to help others and how one can reach deliverance regardless of the level you are on.

Don't get caught up in spending too much time wondering how this happened in your house, to your marriage, to you. Now that you know it's there, put on your armor and fight. When I was into the streets, we used to have this saying before we had a fight; we'd say to the person about to fight, "Buck up," which meant 'guard yourself and get ready for the showdown'.

CHAPTER SEVEN

The Naked Truth

Every law has the ability to be broken regardless of the consequences. And although there comes some very serious repercussions for breaking the law, laws are yet broken without thought every day. This goes way back to when Adam and Eve were in the Garden of Eden and ate of the one tree that God had commanded them not to eat of. Humans have always had the ability to choose because God created us with a free will. Right and wrong, morality and immorality, truth or falsehood, sin or salvation — I can go on and on; we have a choice. Out of all the chapters in this book, this is probably the hardest one to write because of the contents it contains.

There's an old fable that I'd like to share:

One afternoon truth and lie went swimming in the lake. Lie got out first and stole truth's clothes and

disguised himself as the truth. So, when truth got out of the water he discovered that lie had stolen his clothes. When truth arrived into town uncovered, someone asked, "What are you doing?" He replied," I'm just being the naked truth."

The truth of the matter is this: **Everyone** has fallen into the spirit of perversion or sexual immorality on some level and at some point in their life, even those in happy marriages, believe it or not. And I'll prove it. When we hear someone talk about the spirit of perversion, our minds go quickly to the male gender and to either pornography or masturbation. Right? But this spirit goes s-o-o-o much deeper than any of us may think or have been taught.

Remember *Galatians 6:1 says...*

*Brethren, if a man be overtaken in a fault, ye which are spiritual restore such a one in the spirit of meekness ... **considering yourself lest you also be tempted** [emphasis mine].*

Take note of the last part of that scripture because it is very relevant to what God is trying to say: it applies to everyone! And for some this will be a complete shocker. Falling subject to perverse practices is easier than you may think. Modern western society has adopted some perverse customs or practices on one level or another. Let's take a look at Valentine's Day for starters.

Every February 14th People everywhere bombard every store all over this country in preparation for this day that supposedly celebrates love. Some start weeks ahead of time to beat the rush, get the good deals, and avoid the big crowds, all in the name of getting their sweetheart a gift that says "I Love You" in some sort of way. Whether it be balloons of all kinds of shapes and sizes, chocolates treats smooth and sweet to the taste with decadent creaminess, flowers by the bundle wrapped in ribbons and lace, cards, expensive jewelry of gold and diamonds — we go crazy preparing for this day of "love" – but could it be more like a day of lust, especially considering how many of us buy the sexiest lingerie we can find made of mesh in the brightest reds and softest pinks in anticipation of the hot night of lust and passion we'll share together. Right? We head to the novelty shops and indulge in buying all kinds of creams, lotions, oils, and sex toys. We even have our children caught up in this day of love that has worldwide observance. I can remember bugging my mother to buy my Valentine's Day cards so I could give them out to my classmates when I was in elementary school, cards that said stuff like "will you be mine" with a picture of cupid and all that jazz. We literally go broke spending our last dollar to make our significant other feel appreciated on this day. All of us are guilty of doing this; no on is exempt. Oh gosh! And if we don't get a gift we're ready to tear somebody's head off. I was often guilty of that one ... until God revealed to me what I'm about to reveal to you in a minute. The naked truth is that historically, Valentine's Day was a pagan holiday that was celebrated with orgies and sexual perversion. This widespread "day of love" has absolutely nothing to do with love at all in its origin.

Are you sitting down for this?

Centuries before Jesus Christ came on the scene, the Romans had a festival which they celebrated on February 14 in honor of their god called "the hunter of wolves" who went by the name "lupercus." This was an idolatrous and perverted festival filled with *ménage a trios* sexual liaisons of all kinds. Fornication was big at this time of celebration for the Romans and it was permitted for teenagers to take part as well.

During this time of year there was a threat of wolves that would wander around and invade pastures and areas where the shepherds kept their flocks. And the god by the name of lupercus (the hunter of wolves) was believed by the people to watch and protect these flocks and herdsman at night from these vicious animals. So to show their appreciation for the supposed protection given by lupercus (baal), the people would have a feast in honor of this pagan god. During this sexual fiesta the names of young women were placed into a box of some kind and picked out by men to have sex with on this day. And the young lady whose name a man chose was given a formal invitation (by the man) to this orgy that read something like, "Will you be mine?"

Sound familiar? This is where the giving of the cards came from.

According to the Greek, another name for lupercus is "baul or baal" (or could be baal) and this pertains to any idol god in the Old Testament by other cultures (according to a Modern Greek dictionary) any an all idol gods were referred to as baal. The Bible refers to baal in many different Old Testament scriptures as the object of idol worship, which can be translated to "nimrod" (the "Might Hunter") in

Genesis 10:9

> *He was a mighty hunter before the Lord; therefore it is said like nimrod a mighty hunter before the Lord.*

Among the people, nimrod was a great man. According to Scripture he was the first truly mighty man in the earth … and he was everything except holy. He was *not* a lover of God; in fact, he purposely went against everything God stood for. He was viewed as many different things, and thus he was identified by many different names, such as *cupid*, which means "desired" — who is the idol god of love. In fact, he was so desired by women that he was also lusted after by his own mother and was wed by her.

Many believe he was the image referred to in *Ezekiel 8:3-5* as the "idol of jealousy":

> *The Spirit lifted me up between earth and heaven and in visions of God he took me to Jerusalem, to the entrance to the north gate of the inner court, where the idol that provokes to jealousy stood. And there before me was the glory of the God of Israel, as in the vision I had seen in the plain.*
> *Then he said to me, "Son of man, look toward the north." So I looked, and in the entrance north of the gate of the altar I saw this idol of jealousy.*

You can read further on the activities of nimrod, but according to some biblical historians he was born on January 6, and in those days it was customary for a woman to stay inside for forty days after giving birth to a child before she and her newborn child could be considered purified and thus accepted into society. According to our modern calendar, forty days from January 6 is February 14. Thus, the Romans chose February 14 to celebrate this "hunter of the wolf" god.

So, do you still want those flowers and candy? In anticipation of this gala of fornication and perversion, the symbol of love (the shape of a heart with an arrow through it) was passed among the people in anticipation of this paganistic day. The symbol of the heart represented love, and the arrow signified the bow and arrow that was used for hunting the wolves.

Some even believe that once a wolf was killed, its heart was cut out and an arrow was shot through it, and now that's a very familiar symbol we use in today's society to depict love.

If you take the time to research your history you will find that this is the true origin of Valentine's Day, supposedly the "day of love."

Truth be told, the *real* symbol of love is the *cross* upon which Christ was crucified and died for all mankind on Calvary. He took the sins of the whole world so that we can be reconciled back to the Father. Now we all have the ability to bask in real love.

The day that Christ died for us is the real Day of Love and not Valentines' day, and the Cross is the symbol of love not a heart with an arrow going through it.

Now let's take an honest look at sexual immorality, shall we?

Let marriage be held honorable among all, and let the marriage be undefiled; for God will judge the immoral and the adulterous (Hebrews 13:4 Revised Standard KJV).

For years we have been mislead to the meaning of this particular scripture. So many are afraid to teach and speak on what are the right and the wrong way to engage in sexual intercourse within a (Christian) marriage. We have been led to believe that as long as two people are married then all sexual activity is justified by their vow of marriage. Yes marriage should be honorable in all because God ordained marriage and anything He puts into fruition should be honored; don't you agree? But here's the deception not from God but from our own selves. Something that was God created as respectable and upright we have perverted by adopting the worlds way of sexual gratification. Instead of debating whether this may or may not be true, let's shed some light on the situation. Remember when I said that every law has the ability to be broken?

According to *Webster's New World Dictionary and Thesaurus*, the word "**honor**" or "**honorable**" means "praiseworthy, principled, respectable, proper, moral, upright, bringing honor, and/or to adhere to principles considered to be right.

In keeping with the Greek and Hebrew translations, **Aminantos** or "undefiled" means *free from contamination*. **Miano** means *to defile* or *pollute*. This word specifically denotes having the ability to be changed from one aspect to another; in other words, from undefiled to defile.

Sexual intercourse was created to be beautiful before the Lord, because this act was meant to produce more sons of

God in the earth and thus extending His lineage. But we have corrupted this coming together because of a lack of knowledge and due to fear.

We have adopted some practices that are against the sole purpose of reproduction and ***honorable pleasure.***

Let's take a look at what *Leviticus 18:23 says:*

> *Neither shall thou lay with any beast to defile thyself wherewith: neither shall any woman stand before a beast to lie down thereto:*
> *it is confusion.*

"Doggy style" is a sexual position that is very common nowadays when engaging in sexual intercourse between spouses. Of course we are aware that having sexual intercourse with an animal is vile, ungodly, and immoral to say the least, and many of you would detest indulging in an act so odious as that. Am I right? God created animals and humans to be distinct, even in reproduction. Only animals were created to mate in that manner; God didn't intend for humans to adopt the practice of animals, although some evolutionists would like for us to believe that we all came from apes. That is in no way truth; that's just another ploy of the enemy trying to remove God (and His pre-eminence) out of creation. We were created by God with a plan in mind; we were created in His image in the flesh with a living soul. But at some point in time someone somewhere saw two animals mating and was sexually aroused by what they witnessed, and so they brought this idea into the bedroom. And that spirit was born, fed, grew, and now it is so widespread it's evident in almost every bedroom in this country. And this is a type of the spirit of *Bestiality.* No, I'm not saying you're having sex *with* an animal, but you are having sex *like* an animal. *How do you think that position got its name?* Many people would get offended if you were to call them a dog, which in today's society means they are a player or a gigolo. According to the New Testament being called a dog meant that you were the minority (read the story about the Syro Phoenician woman.) But how is it that people don't like to be referred to as a dog but they don't mind having sex like one? How can God get the glory out of that?

Now let's take a look at *Romans 1:26-27:*

Because of this, God gave them over to shameful lusts. Even their women exchanged natural relations for unnatural ones. In the same way the men also abandoned natural relations with women and were inflamed with lust for one another. Men committed indecent acts with other men, and received in themselves the due penalty for their perversion.

Anal and oral sex is another one that many people try to excuse as being normal. There's a very big debate on this subject in the church; therefore, since everyone is discussing it, let me put in my two cents' worth. Again, sex was created by God for reproduction as we already know. But answer this ... How are anal and oral sex a form of reproduction? Both these forms of sex **take away the distinction of gender**, male and female, which makes these acts illicit and unlawful, and they are also a type and shadow of *Homosexuality*. God did not create the anus and mouth for sexual gratification; it does not reproduce. He (God) came down from heaven himself and destroyed two whole cities because of these very same acts, the infamous Sodom and Gomorrah. He could have easily dispatched a few angels to take care of the task but this act was so detesting He did it himself. Now we know that this was not the only reason that the two cities were destroyed but this is clearly one of the reasons. To this day there is no evidence of those two cities having ever existed; they can't be found anywhere except in the Word. So tell me, how does marriage suddenly make these perverse sex acts permissible? Quiet as it's kept; this is a spirit of *Sodomy*.

These are just a few; there are many more. But I'll stop with these two since they are the most common. **I'm not trying to start a sex doctrine amongst believers**. Everyone has a choice, and I'm not trying to take away that choice. However, I am "crying loud and sparing not." My pastor always says that you are responsible for what you know and you will be judged by what you do with that information. There are those who will say, "There's nothing wrong with these types of sexual activities," but be careful, because **that is the spirit**

talking as it tries to defend itself against the Word. God created a law and order for *everything*, even down to the different seasons ... Yes! There's even an order for sex. Yes! You love your mate and you want to do what pleases them but God comes above all and you should *never* go against God and His word to please flesh. Some people may think sex is boring without all these variations, and that they're needed for fun and ultimate pleasure, but if you need immoral performance in order to "spice things up" (as some would say), just know that you don't need these particular practices to do that. Ask God to rekindle your *pure passion* for your mate; indulge in exploring falling in love all over again. That's more than spicy ... that's everlasting. God doesn't want to make your life boring and miserable; **He wants to make it a ministry** ... even in sex (when it's done the right way).

CHAPTER EIGHT

The Weight of Forgiveness

The Power of Repentance

It is easy to live life with hidden secrets that no other person may know about; you can just pretend that everything is fine. Dressing up the outside is always the easiest thing to do. But how are you living on the inside? Have you mastered the art of disguise so well that you've disguised yourself even from you?

What hidden thing is destroying you mentally and emotionally and tearing apart your family and your home? Today can be the day when you decide to stop allowing the enemy to trick you as he also tries to minimize your faith in God. Sins that are unforgiven bring separation from your heavenly Father and **death**.

You know what tickles me? Have you ever been to a church that has a testimony service? Listen to all the stuff that is said. We don't mind other people knowing that God delivered us from drugs, fighting, drinking, smoking, and stealing, *those are the popular sins* because it places in the minds of the listener that you were no joke but no one ever wants to confess the bondage of a perverse spirit. I have heard some who were bold enough to confess this, but very few. If you have read "The Naked Truth" chapter then you know that everyone has fallen to a perverse spirit or practice on some level at some point in their lives.

Confessing sin is **never** easy, especially if you have covered it up for so long or if what you have to say is embarrassing. But allow me to let you in on something: our churches are filled with hurting people, and messed-up people can only relate to those who have been messed up but have also been healed. Isn't that ironic? What would church be like if all the churchgoers felt ashamed and kept their secrets or their deliverance testimonies to themselves? No one else would be encouraged to get delivered. That's why getting delivered is so imperative your testimony is not for you as much as it is for those who are listening. Someone's destiny lies in your testimony. What would happen to those who want to be free but feel like they can't because there is no one they can relate to? They leave the church because they feel that no one understands them and what they're struggling with.

There is tremendous power in repentance.

He that covereth his sins shall not prosper: but whoso confesseth and forsaketh them shall have mercy. Happy is the man that feareth always: but he that hardeneth his heart shall fall into mischief

(Proverbs 28:13-14).

If you are a pastor or a church leader (struggling) reading this book and you're thinking, *well I certainly can't confess my sins publicly*, because of the position that you are in please know that I can understand why this would be difficult for you, holding the office that you hold but it's important to understand that *No One* is exempt from the rules. And those in leadership positions are the first partakers of the fruit. Find a colleague in the spirit that can **help** and **handle** your confession. The reason I say handle is because everyone is not equipped to mentally manage your secret battles, some people have not learned to separate the two (the person from the spirit). My dad used to say you can't judge a man's anointing by what he does in the flesh. Some people don't know how to cope with that. On another note there's always the factor of you and God; either way it must be done. God can heal any and everyone, including you. He wants to heal you! He's a God of restoration; that's His forte´. And if you are a worker in the vineyard

(Regardless to what magnitude), imagine how much more powerful your ministry will be once you repent and come to full deliverance?

Of course, we were taught that if we say, "Lord, forgive me of all my sins," that covers them all. That may be true, but it still doesn't hurt to repent for specific sins. Let's take a look at the story of the prodigal son for a moment.

> *And when he came to himself, he said, How many hired servants of my father's have bread enough and to spare, and I perish with hunger. I will arise and go to my father, and will say unto him, Father, I have sinned against heaven, and before thee. And am no more worthy to be called thy son: make me as one of thy hired servants*
> *(Luke 15:17-19).*

The prodigal son knew what he had done and wanted full forgiveness. And he knew that in order to do that he had to **specifically address** that **particular** sin for which he wanted to be forgiven. Imagine if he had merely said, "Father, forgive me for all my sins." Although his father knew what he had done and to what he would have been referring, that sin needed clarity because such a generic request could be referring to the time he was playing ball in the house. He had to take away the possibility of misinterpretation; thus the need for specific repentance.

As I referred to this passage about the prodigal son I asked myself, *what was it about him that made him a prodigal?* We oftentimes believe that he was prodigal because he left home and spent all his inheritance foolishly, but after some research I found that this was only part of the scenario.

The word prodigal means reckless, spoiled, extravagant; lush, profuse. In one dictionary it also means **rebellious**, which in the Old Testament was punishable by death as described in *Deuteronomy 21:18*.

According to *Deuteronomy 21:15-16*, the prodigal son went against the law given to Moses. According to custom it was disrespectful for a son to ask for his inheritance before the father died (or was dying). An inheritance was to be given at or near the time of the father's death. Secondly, the youngest son was not to get his inheritance before the eldest son, so that was two whammies in one but his cockiness preceded him. And when He said that he had sinned against heaven and his father; he knew that he had gone against the law and that he had disrespected his father. It had nothing to do with his spending habits. Those things described in his character are a description of a spirit. Or in other words, he was called prodigal because he had a reckless, rebellious and spoiled spirit. He was rebellious against the law. The Bible said that he was the youngest, and we know that the youngest children – the babies of families — are usually spoiled. He could have spent down to his socks (which he did), but it was that which was in his spirit that caused him to be prodigal.

He needed to repent of what he'd done according to what was in his spirit.

Only then was he able to be received by his father as well as forgiven by him.

Gods' love for us is beyond our imagination. Repentance determines where you spend eternity. That's why God sent his Son in the flesh to be crucified on the cross for your sins, because repentance is a very important part of forgiveness and salvation. God will forgive you, but you must be willing to repent.

The Weight of Forgiveness

"Forgiveness is easier said than done, **but it's better done than said.**"

> *For if ye forgive men their trespasses, your heavenly Father will also forgive you.*
>
> *But if ye forgive not men their trespasses, neither will your Father forgive your trespasses (Matthew 6:14-15).*

Forgiveness is a very powerful tool, and once you are able to forgive ... *then* you can be forgiven.

How much you put up with in a *"prodigal"* spouse is totally up to you. I definitely believe that God can deliver anyone. But you (the praying spouse) must be willing to endure the extra heartache you may face until your mate receives total deliverance. You must grab hold of faith and believe that total breakthrough is on the way. Most deliverance does not take place overnight, and things may seem to get worse before they get better. Some must endure a little longer, but take comfort; your help is on the way.

The righteous cry, and the Lord heareth, and delivereth them out of all their troubles.

The Lord is nigh unto them that are of a broken heart; and saveth such as be of a contrite spirit.

Many are the afflictions of the righteous; but the Lord delivereth him out of them all (Psalms 34:17-19).

Forgiveness is a very imperative part of salvation; without it no one can see God. Jesus came to take every sin of all mankind to the cross. Forgiveness is giving up resentment and refusing the desire to punish. Is forgiveness a hard thing to do? In some cases, yes! Some things are easier to forgive than others but it **must** be done. There is *no* way around that. My father used to say, "Forgiveness is not for the other person; *it's for you.*"

We've all heard that we should "forgive and forget." I've always wondered *how you do that*. We have a memory box in our brains that was designed for us to distinctively remember some things. I'm inclined to believe differently from that saying of "forgive and forget," because there were some wrongs done to me that I will never forget. God forbid but if someone shot you no matter how saved you are you'll never forget the shooting or the person that did it. Which in my opinion has no bearing if you are a true saint or not. If we all just forgot the bad stuff in our lives where would the testimonies come from? Some people believe that if you don't forget that you haven't forgiven but I disagree. Forgiveness is determined on your desire for punishment from that particular wrong. Or if you are still seeking judgment for what that individual has done. But because of the measure of grace and mercy that was unselfishly given to me by almighty God, I must show forth that same compassion toward others.

Forgiveness must go much further than a person's flippant statement of, "I'm sorry; can you forgive me?" It is a critical part of how we view the Word of God. It says that we give up our own will and succumb to what God desires of us no matter how hard it may be. Now that's Sonship.

> *Then Peter to him, and said, Lord, how oft shall my brother sin against me, and I forgive him? Till seven times? Jesus said unto him, I say not unto thee,*

Until seven times: but seventy times seven (Matthew 18:21-22).

Let me put it like this: *Ima be real wich cha'*. I know how hard it is to forgive. And anyone who tells you "Oh, it's always easy" isn't being totally truthful. But *choose* to please God and He will vindicate you. Imagine how hard it must have been for the prophet Hosea to take back his wife, but he realized he was not his own, and Gods' will must be above anything he felt. (Refer to the chapter "Not a "G" Thang.")

There will always be consequences for our actions, but there is no sin that can't be forgiven unless you're dealing with blasphemy against the Holy Spirit.

Repentance and forgiveness need to take place from three aspects:

1) **Repentance from the bound-up believer to God the Father.** When you are truly sorry with godly sorrow and you go to God in true repentance, He can, will, and is always ready to forgive you. And once you have repented and have been forgiven by the Father, then the second aspect of repentance must take place... And this is where you must forgive yourself. Don't allow the enemy to mentally beat you down. God is the ultimate and once He forgives you no one can hold anything against you, even you.

3) **Repentance and forgiveness must take place between spouses** from one spouse to the other. This is not a one-sided thing; this needs to be done on a mutual basis, not just one spouse apologizing and the other accepting. There needs to be a corporate communication here to cover all bases so that there is **no** door left open for the devil to creep back in on another level.

When you're being asked for forgiveness or when you want to be forgiven, take into account all the times you needed forgiveness from God or someone else. In situations that call for forgiveness on some level, always remember your own shortcomings *no matter what side of the fence you're on.*

CHAPTER NINE

When the Lights Go Out

This chapter is written specifically for the person who is bound by sexual perversion (though all can read it). Not only those who struggle with masturbation or pornography but any one of the perversions that was mentioned in *chapter two*. In this chapter we will talk about the changing of behavior: doing things differently and starting over. Old habits are hard to break, and you feel like you're caught in the middle between the strengths of two powers fighting against one another. One is right and the other is satisfying. The reason that I titled this chapter "When the Lights Go Out" is because the times will come when you will be faced with these ungodly desires and no one will be there but you and God: the times when you're home alone, there's nothing good on television, everyone has gone to the movies or out to eat, your mate is at work, and the children are over at a neighbor's house.

It's easy to be in a church service where the spirit is moving, everybody's clapping, and crying, the pastor is laying on hands and people are falling out by the power of God. Your emotions are heightened and you feel that you can beat every demon and devil that comes your way you're 'amped up and ready for battle. But when you're alone and the light's lights go out, what do you do then?

And be not conformed to this world; but be ye transformed by the renewing of your mind, that ye may prove what is that good, and acceptable, and perfect, will of God (Romans 12:2).

Renouncing is not enough; the fight now becomes harder, not that it wasn't difficult already. Referring back to knowing your weapons of warfare is critical at this point, because you're going to need them. You must take in the Word of God and understand some key elements and behavior that must now become evident in your walk with God.

Key elements:
- Character
- Integrity
- Nobility
- Persona
- Morality

Your mindset needs to be retrained and redirected to what is right and righteous. You have to first recognize who and what you are in Christ. When you accept salvation you are no longer a prisoner to the enemy and sin; instead you have been grafted into the faith, by faith. This gives you power over the spirit that is tempting you to defile your body, which is the temple of the Holy Spirit. But you must first realize and understand the power and authority you have over this lust, which was given to you by Jesus Christ. And with authority comes the obligation to do what is right. *Matthew 16:19* says, *"And I will give you the keys of the kingdom of heaven, and whatever you bind on earth will be bound in heaven, and whatever you loose on earth will be loosed in heaven."* You must begin to walk in your God-given authority. Right here at this place of your greatest temptation is where you need to bind every thought, every ungodly feeling, and every wicked imagination that would exalt itself above the Word of God.

Years ago I heard a message preached, and one thing the preacher said has stuck with me until this day, and I use it in my prayers when I pray. She said that "once we close the door we must seal it behind us."

Doors are used for entering and exiting. And once you opened and then closed the door to that spirit, now you must **Seal It!** Remember when I talked about furnishing your empty places with the Word of God? My pastor taught us that once we receive the Holy Spirit we have the power to activate and loose the anointing of God into the atmosphere.

When you speak in authority against these spirits that have you bound, you weaken their hold on you. And after a while they loosen their grip. And have to completely let go.

Let's break down the five key elements to changing behavior.

Character - The pattern of behavior or personality found in an individual.

This denotes having a good, moral reputation to such an extent that people are able to speak well of your nature. How you carry yourself and your attributes ... how you are by natural behavior. Or how you are viewed based on your actions and reactions.

Integrity - The state of being sound, moral, principled; uprightness, honesty, and sincerity.

This is easy to do when you are in front of other people, but integrity is living like your life is on the front page every second of every day. This is where what you do when you're alone counts. It's like if a person never cleans their house. When nobody knows that your house is dirty then there is no problem, but when everyone knows that you're a nasty person then the shame hits home. And this is what integrity is, it's doing what's right when you're alone and nobody can see you.

Nobility - Showing high moral qualities; greatness of character; having superior qualities.

When you are noble other people can expect honesty and a passion for from you. You become and place yourself in a place of being well respected among others that know you or know of you. You are admired for your qualities and your character sings your praises. People are compelled to tribute your good nature.

Persona - The outer personality presented to others by an individual.

Your persona is where you represent Christ. And what kind of lifestyle you live before the world, especially those who are not saved. How do you carry yourself? How are you viewed as a person by the people around you? Would your neighbors be shocked to find out that you are a Christian? Or how do you act when you're out in the public eye? Are you friendly or do people think you have a bad attitude? Are you loud and rowdy or do you walk in the spirit of soberness? Those who live with you count too.

And...

Morality - A mindset characterized by courage, discipline, confidence, and the willingness to endure hardship.

I like the way the word "discipline" is used here. You have to be able to control your flesh. Your spirit should control your flesh and not your flesh is in control of you. You can get that flesh under subjection by the power of God. When you're tempted by lusts you need to say, "No! Flesh, we're not doing that today." And repeat it the next day tell it again, until it's imparted in your spirit and it's finally conquered. Then you'll start to be in control of your flesh, and your flesh will not be in control of you.

God's plan and predestination of human events does not eliminate human choice. Every one is accountable for their actions. I know some church people who willingly sin, and when questioned about it they'll say, "I'm not delivered in that area yet." Or, "I haven't been delivered from that yet." But that doesn't take away God's power to deliver. Those are the sins we want to hang on to and not even try to let go of. God's power is mighty enough to deliver us from all old habits no matter what they may be. But we must come to a place within ourselves where we no longer desire to house these ungodly spirits. And we must stop excusing what we do by trying to implicate that God isn't who He says He is. If we curse and speak in tongues out of our same mouth, we can't say "put that on God" weakening His power to deliver. We do it because we want to, or else we haven't come to the place where we truly want to let that go. This is an area where we'll say, "Well, no one knows what Paul's thorn in the flesh was." Imagine what it would be like if we did know. Everybody would do "that" particular thing and fight to justify it tooth and nail. Remember what I said about placing ourselves in the same league with the great Apostle Paul, or trying to use the scripture to justify our sins, so I'm not even going there. I've got to make it for myself and so do you. That's why it is so imperative to allow God to transform your mind. When those weak moments come; talk to your Father right then and there. I know the urge is hard to fight, but don't fight in the flesh; fight in the spirit. Remember what it means to live in integrity. Don't give up.

I remember the Sunday when the deliverance took place in my marriage. I'll never forget that day. Our pastor had called an altar call for deliverance lots of people went to the alter, getting deliverance from all kinds of things. Many were crying and repenting and asking the Lord for forgiveness. And then my pastor came down and laid hands on my husband, and she began to come against spirits with the weight of the anointing. The spirit of God was so high in that service, people were getting delivered from all kinds of things that day. My husband had kneeled to the ground in surrender, and my pastor got on her knees right there alongside him (kneeling in her nice robe), and as long as he stayed down there she stayed there right beside him. She made sure the enemy knew that he wasn't having my husband's mind without a fight. I will always love her for that.

I shared that for this reason: the theme for that particular Sunday was to come to terms with whatever sin or spirit people were dealing with. There were a lot of people at the altar that day, so it made coming to terms with your issue a lot easier because everybody was up there. But after the music, and the clapping, and the anointing with oil, and the pastor nowhere near by at this point, we had to make up in our mind that the battle was over on that Sunday, and any thing that came after that we was going to fight.

Flee also youthful lust: but follow righteousness, faith, charity, peace, with them that call on the Lord out of a pure heart (Timothy 2:22).

CHAPTER TEN

Healing for Your Soul

Just as deliverance is a process, so is healing. But God is there ready and willing to heal both spouses. Healing is a must when you're dealing with issues that can ultimately break up a family. Repentance, forgiveness, sensitivity, communication, and honesty are very critical to this process. So much has been damaged but not destroyed. Building a strong foundation in the beginning of a relationship is so vital because of the different levels of disaster a storm can bring later in life. But as you build a firm foundation, you always have the potential to rebuild, and when you do, this time you can build a stronger place than before. In the previous chapter we covered repentance and forgiveness; now let's deal with honesty, sensitivity, communication, and healing.

*And ye shall know the truth, and the truth shall **make** you free (John 8:32).*

I have heard so many people quote this scripture wrong by saying the truth shall "set" you free. But it says **make**. Here the word *make* refers to being made separate. In other words, the truth will separate you from guilt.

Honesty is so crucial here because there is a level of dependency that needs to be rebuilt. And if you can't be honest without fear of backlash, the trust can never be restored. Both spouses need to be able to come to each other and be honest about the things that have taken place, as well as share how it made them feel, exposing everything! Best friends are supposed to be able to tell each other everything without fear. Those hidden things need to be dealt with, even if they conjure up old feelings for a moment. Both parties may feel uncomfortable about really expressing their hurts and concerns in fear that this conversation may turn into an arguing match. But let's deal with this differently. Let's not engage in conversation; let's *indulge* in communication.

Open **communication** means that we both get time on the table to share whatever it is we are feeling without rebuttal, and that we are able to have our deepest feelings heard without fear of critical remarks. Communication says *I don't fear you not agreeing to listen to what I have to say.* It says, *Together we will face, in truth and honesty, how we made each other feel.* It is unfair to your spouse when you aren't completely honest with them, because they deserve to know what is going on in their relationship with you. You take away their power to be equivalent when you're not honest. Why should you know something about your relationship and your spouse does not?

Honesty not only says *I can depend on you to be true to me,* but it also says, *whenever I have an issue I can come to you and not be reluctant about it.* **Make time** to really communicate with one another. Take the children over to grandma's and allow no company, no phone, no television — just you and your spouse. Bring your tissue and every emotion and lay it all on the line. It may get a little heated because you're dealing with a touchy subject (for both spouses). But remember no yelling. This is not shouting match. If shouting does began to be a factor in the communication process be mature enough to leave the table express and the necessity for a mental break once has been re-established return to continue. Calm and sober. Don't think the spouse that was bound by the spirit of perversion is not hurt by their actions, because any true child of God is hurt by sinful actions. Whether they admit it or not, they realize that not only have they hurt you, but they have sinned against the God whom they love. So remember they are hurting to. One thing that needs to be done to eliminate all kinds of chaos first of all is **prayer**! Before you come together to talk, pray and bind any occurrences that will cause your communication time to be ineffectual. And don't let your mate do all the apologizing. Both parties must realize that both are hurting. I can't stress that enough.

Note: Be aware of how you communicate and take a note on how you express your feelings in high intense situations especially if you have children. Because how you openly display your anger will be exemplified in your children, thus you teach them how to communicate and express their anger. So let's say that every time you get mad you start to throw stuff and begin to scream to the top of your voice, if you display that type of behavior in front of your children, they will then begin to compute and process in their minds that this is how to express them self when they are feeling angry. And they will begin to demonstrate how they feel in the same manner, thinking that this is how anger is supposed to be expressed and how I get my emotions identified.

Here are some good tips to help you communicate better:

Don't go to the communication table ready to judge, this is not a court hearing. Judging and pointing the finger will only make things worse. There should be no dominant party, with one out-talking the other. **Share the conversation**. It may get a little lengthy, but remember, you're talking about your marriage, and not everything has a quick fix! You should want to take your time when you're dealing with something so delicate. Be willing to listen. The key to being a good conversationalist is being a good listener. Listen with your heart, not just your ears; don't be so ready to get your point across. Hear your mate out, and try not to be in such a rush to interject your viewpoint. You can even bring a paper and pen; take notes so that you can revisit a view point that you wanted to address while your mate was talking.

Keep in mind that both individuals have issues and concerns that have evolved over time as a result of this. **Sensitivity** needs to be extended on both parts. When it came time to address the issue on an emotional level, my husband and I prayed for wisdom on how to address the issue and each other. And when you're dealing with a human being, their emotions are not to be taken lightly. Some people take so seriously how you've made them feel that they retaliate in sometimes violent behavior. It's actually very common that people don't know how to deal with their emotions and what they are feeling. That's why sensitivity is another important part of healing. Have you ever been so passionate about something, and the person you're sharing your passion with showed an attitude while listening to you like they couldn't care less? Remember how that made you feel and the feelings of frustration it brought when you thought you were being taken lightly?

> *But thou, O Lord, art a God*
> *full of compassion, and gracious, longsuffering, and*
> *plenteous in mercy and truth*
> *(Psalms 86:15).*

Although this scripture is speaking of God, we too can also adopt these same attributes when dealing with one another.

The Bible also refers to *compassion*, which is another word for sensitivity. It was important that I not only heard what my husband had to say but to understand how he felt as well; and him vice-versa. I needed to be sensitive because it was imperative for him to know that I was hearing him with my heart. Sensitivity calls for the spirit of discernment. It can be damaging to a person's emotions when they're not being understood emotionally. That's why you hear a lot of people say "No one understands me". It's not that they're so peculiar that they can't be understood by anyone else. I guarantee that if you sat them down and asked them if someone has actually taken the time to talk to them about how they feel (and literally take into consideration their feelings), it'll probably take them a while to think back. We all need the reassurance that the person to whom we are speaking is really listening to how we are feeling. And because we take ample time to discuss our issues and concerns, we don't have to sit down every week and revisit the same issues over and over. That's wasted time that could be better spent moving on in the Lord.

There are so many instances in the scriptures where God has healed somebody, from sicknesses and diseases, to healing those who are crippled and mute, but God's ability to heal certainly doesn't stop there. He has healed hearts and marriages since the beginning of time. And as long as humans are emotional beings, we need God to be in the healing business. Emotional pains and setbacks are inevitable in this life ... but there is a refuge.

CHAPTER ELEVEN

Not a "G" Thang

Let's deal with this in brief, because this is really self-explanatory.

Often when we think of the spirit of perversion our mind immediately goes straight to the male gender and we're ready for the attack. But the truth of the matter is that spirits attach themselves to **whoever** is open and venerable, male or female. I can recall one of the discussions that with one of the couples dealing with perversion; in this instance it was a pastor whose wife was bound by the spirit of perversion, he went on to describe the different things that he had to deal with in his household. The scripture says that *"we wrestle not against flesh and blood but against principalities in high places."* When dealing with the female gender, you also have to recognize the emotional connection a female may have as opposed to the male species. Although most males that deal with this vile passion may be dealing with it on a pleasure level or for sexual gratification, females are emotional creatures by nature. Spirits attack homes no matter whose home it is or who in the household it may hurt.

When I titled this chapter "Not a "G" Thang" I was alluding not only to the **gender** point of view but also to having a **godly** point of view. When a Syro-Phoenician woman came to Jesus, on behalf of her daughter, saying:

> *Have mercy on me, O Lord, thou*
> *son of David; my daughter is grievously vexed*
> *with a devil (Matthew 15:22).*

Spirits latch on to girls too. I'm not making light of the situation by referring to it as a "G" thang, but it's time that we got out of this stereotypical mindset that ungodly lustful spirits only attach themselves to the male gender. This is so far from the truth; in fact, there are some females who are more pernicious than males these days.

Sexual gratification as opposed to ungodly soul ties are on two different levels.

And although women are as susceptible as men, women sometimes get locked in a lot of times through ungodly soul ties in some cases because we lock into emotion. Now the action of some of the women in the Bible was very risqué. Because you are still dealing with a time when women were trained and taught to be subservient, meek, and self-effacing.

And anything out of this sort/class was unheard of for women in most instances in those times.

Hosea 1:1-5

Let's look at the prophet Hosea and **Gomer** his wife. Although this union was an open demonstration of how God felt about the children of Israel, it doesn't take away from the natural fact that Gomer was this man's wife with whom he had children. I imagine he loved her very much as any man of God should love his wife. And she was an adulteress. For this act according to the law she could have been stoned to death. She was the symbol chosen for Israel's' infidelity against God. What a position she had to occupy.

Genesis 39:1-13 tells the story of Potiphar's wife.

Potiphar's wife was bound by a spirit of lust; she wanted to sleep with Joseph so badly that she was obsessive about it. The scriptures tell us how she tried to verbally seduce him day after day, repeatedly asking him to take her until one day she got bold enough to grab him. Don't forget when dealing in the Bible times you're referring to an era in history when the women were supposed to be as humble and as quiet as lambs, with a walk so light as to almost not be heard and a voice so soft it was almost a whisper.

These are a few mentioned just to substantiate to the fact that the spirits are indifferent. There are many examples of women who were overtaken by ungodly spirits. There are just as many women in the sex industry today as there are men. And as hard as it is to believe, women rape too. So let's get away from always thinking that the men are the only ones who battle with the spirit of perversion.

Then we can also refer to **The Women at the well** who met up with Jesus and he began to speak to her concerning her issue. He asked her where her husband was, and she answered him saying I have none. Some have said that she was bound by *adultery* and others have said that she was bound by *fornication*. The truth of the matter is this; she may not have been bound by either. She may have been dealing with a heavy spirit of rejection and or loneliness that caused her to have so many different relationships. Remember what I said earlier about looking for approval when you feel rejected? Rejection and depression causes for the need of affirmation, confirmation, and attention. Though this desire for attention for what ever reason is unhealthy it causes you to act out of the spirit of desperation. And you'll find yourself in relationship after relationship looking for love in all the wrong places. However you look at it, before she met with Jesus she was bound by something that needed Gods' attention. There are a few more women that I could name in this chapter but I think you get the picture.

So with that being said- always remember a spirit latches to whomever makes themselves available. Regardless of your gender, whether you may be young or old. Or no matter what side of the fence you are on. There is always healing for all, be encouraged in the Lord.

Seek the Lord while He may be found,
Call ye upon Him while he is near.

Let the wicked forsake his way, and the unrighteous
man his thoughts:
And let him return unto the Lord, and he will have
mercy upon him; and to our God,
for he will abundantly pardon.
Isaiah 55:6-7 (KJV)

Powerful Declarations

Scripture tells us that the power of life and death are in the tongue. Here are some powerful declarations that you can use to over come this spirit:

> I decree and declare that I am no longer a puppet to the enemy and the spirit of perversion, in the name of Jesus.
> I renounce any and all kinds of sexual activity in my life that is not like God, in the name of Jesus.
> I renounce any and all wicked imaginations that come to overtake my mind with ungodly thoughts, in the name of Jesus.
> I denounce sexual perversions and cast them out of my life, and I take back my temple for the Master's use, in the name of Jesus.
> I apply the blood of Jesus to the atmospheric demons that cause my mind to wander toward ungodly thoughts.

I am a son (daughter) of God. I am of the Sent One. I am not a bastard, and I speak deliverance into my life, in the name of Jesus.

I speak restoration to my home, for me and for my spouse, in the name of Jesus.

I declare healing in my body from the crown of my head to the soles of my feet, in the name of Jesus.

I will be whole so that I can fulfill my divine assignment, in the name of Jesus.

I will not live a life of double standards but instead a life that carries spiritual weight, in Jesus' name.

As a son (daughter) of God I have status on the earth. Therefore I will no longer defile my temple with ungodly lust, in Jesus' name.

I will now begin to see myself as God sees me, and I will begin to treat my body as the temple of God, in Jesus' name.

BE BLESSED!

Whatever your struggles may be, confess them to the Lord. If you are unsure of what to say, try this:

Confession Prayer

Heavenly Father...

I confess lying.

I confess cheating.

I confess sexual perversion.

I confess masturbation.

I confess ungodly imaginations.

I confess the addiction to pornography.

I confess the wandering eye.

I confess having froward and wayward conversation.

I confess any thought that would come to exalt itself above God and His Word.

I rebuke the spirit of perversion over my life (my mate's life).

I rebuke the desire for corrupt sexual gratifications.

I recognize this wrong and today I walk in freedom.

Against Thee have I sinned and done this evil in Thy sight. Forgive me, oh Lord, that I may walk blameless before Thee. I no longer want to be bound by the spirit of perversion. Clean me and wash me, Lord, that I may be fit for your use without shame. I change today, Father. I give up the grounds. Give me the mind to be totally free. Help me, Lord, to keep your ordinances and commandments. Keep me, God, when I get weak, and help me to stand against the tricks of the enemy. I need you to help me, Lord, and if you will be with me, I know I'll overcome. In Jesus' name, Amen.

Prayer and Proclamation

Father, in the name of Jesus we come against every thought that is not like you. Forgive us for every sexual sin, oh God! Forgive us for every time we defile our temple with ungodly lust, for in us is where your spirit dwells. We tear down every ungodly and wicked imagination in the name of Jesus. God, we know that you are a healer of hearts, minds, and marriages. Heal us now, God. Touch the lives of your people everywhere who are battling with the spirit of perversion. For we are your people, and we decree and declare everywhere the freedom of your sons and daughters. Touch us as only you can, God. Bring peace to every home. Peace to every heart. And healing to every marriage. Satan, we bind you in the name of Jesus. We rebuke you and all your tactics in the name of Jesus. We plead and apply the blood of Jesus against you now, and we cast you into dry places never to return again, in Jesus' name. Lord, give your people the mind to be free all around this country. We bind embarrassment; the stopper of ministries has been stopped. For every father, every mother, every woman, and every man we reclaim their minds back to you, in the name of Jesus. We loose the spirit of nobility. We will perpetuate the name of Jesus in the earth. We loose the spirit of integrity and we call for the spirit of morality, in Jesus' name. We call the spirit of peace and freedom now, and we loose and activate the healing power of God everywhere. I call you free, in the name of Jesus, and I declare your success over this spirit, for you are an overcomer. In the matchless name of Jesus Christ, Amen.

To contact Anastasia "Stacie" Peart
you may email her at:

Contact Info:
Anastasia Peart
http://manifoldglory@yahoo.com
or log on to: www.manifoldglory.net

Testimonials Welcome

Powerful Reads and Materials:

The Spirit of Aquarius
Written by: Dr. Apostle Aretha Wilson

Sonship, The Weight and Glory
Written by: Dr. Apostle Aretha Wilson

Or log on to: www.rawinternationalministries.org
and click on to: Kingdom Media

Humble Heart Fellowship Ministries
Dr. Apostle Aretha Wilson, Pastor, Presiding prelate and Chief Overseer

Recommended Messages:
The Power of Clothing
A Higher Law

The Power of a Seed
Acquire the Rain
Expose' on Mystery Babylon
A Christmas Story

CPSIA information can be obtained at www.ICGtesting.com
224676LV00001B/178/P